POETRY
FROM THE WINDOWS
OF MY MIND

Author Melvin Hughes

ISBN: 069223182X
ISBN-13: 9780692231821

DEDICATION

This book is dedicated to the many thousands of poetry lovers all over the world who cherish the poetic spoken and written word.

"POETRY FROM THE WINDOWS OF MY MIND " is designed to give rise to provocative thought into the windows of your own inner self, and to even encourage <u>You</u> to consider entering the arena of writing, and bringing to the world your own creative thinking and writing style.

Are you a writer? Sure you are. We all have a story to tell. How good your story is, will depend on the opinions of your readers but the end of any road starts at its beginning.

So don't be afraid. Put it on paper. You will never know if you are good unless you ask. But, rest assured, if you don't ask, the answer is always no.

So, I trust you will enjoy my writing, and I will be waiting for yours.

The Author
Melvin L. Hughes

PREFACE

I have always wanted to write a book, a poem, a song, or anything that had to do with writing. That has always been a dream of mine. It was a dream, but I never really thought I'd do it.

Sometimes we get in the way of our own success, and it takes someone else to point out the possibility of that dream becoming a reality.

Friends and family have often told me, "With all that you have been through in your life, you should write a book." "You've got some stories to tell." I listened and mainly just shrugged it off.

When I entered college, (at age 42) my test scores indicated that I needed developmental English as one of my prerequisites. However, when my instructor saw my first paper he asked; "What are you doing in my class?" "Your English is fine and you write very well." He said," You are a terrible speller, but your editor will handle that."

I was both surprised and pleased at that comment because, even though I started writing poems in elementary school and I still write today, I never thought of myself as a writer. I also like to write personalized greeting cards, and musical lyrics, and once, I sent a poetry sample to the Hallmark Greeting Card Company, just to see what would happen.

To my amazement, they responded, even though they don't usually engage freelance writers. That was more than thirty years ago. At that time, I did not see much of a future in verse @ .04 cent a word, so I never followed up. I may have missed a great opportunity. After 30 years, I still have their response.

 I love the sound of words, and I always find myself correcting the grammar of others' even today. Most people are not happy about that, but it seems I just can't help myself.

I was further encouraged to write by the instructor of my <u>Introduction to College Writing</u> course, who said, "Melvin, you are a good writer and you should consider creative writing as a career choice. My field of choose was Electronics Engineering Technology. This was far removed from anything that resembled writing.

The instructor who was a writer himself, (Richard "Dick" Friedrich) also suggested that I could channel my writing toward technical writing. His impression of my work was, "You have a good sense of simple explanation. To put it another way, "You know how to explain stuff." I "Aced" the class."

I always thought my poetry was pretty good, but that was it, pretty good. Now, after all these years, (I am now 73 years old) I have decided to write my first book. I look for you the reader to determine the substance and value of my writing. I hope that you will enjoy "Poetry From The Windows of My Mind" The Author

TABLE OF CONTENTS

PAGE 10	KNOWLEDGE IS POWER
PAGE 12	YOU ARE VERY SPECIAL
PAGE 14	YOUR PLACE IN THE RACE
PAGE 16	TEMPER
PAGE 17	BE TRUE TO YOU
PAGE 18	JUMP, BABY JUMP
PAGE 19	ANGELS WATCHING
PAGE 21	I'M A SOLDIER
PAGE 23	IF JESUS CAME TODAY
PAGE 25	WHEN I WAS THERE
PAGE 27	IF I SHOULD DIE, BEFORE I WAKE
PAGE 29	WHERE IS YOUR FAITH?
PAGE 30	IF YOUR CROSS IS TO HEAVY CARRY MINE
PAGE 32	THANK YOU
PAGE 34	THE ANGEL VOICE
PAGE 36	I TOLD MY FRIEND TO PRAY
PAGE 38	I LOST MY FRIEND TODAY
PAGE 39	DON'T FORGET TO PRAY
PAGE 40	EVERY DAY AIN'T PRETTY
PAGE 41	KATRINA
PAGE 43	LET'S HAVE ANOTHER HONEYMOON
PAGE 45	HAPPY BIRTHDAY
PAGE 46	THE FAMILY REUNION
PAGE 47	THE THINGS I NEVER SAID
PAGE 48	TOMORROW MIGHT BE TOO LATE
PAGE 49	I'M SORRY
PAGE 50	ME AND MY FRIEND GIN
PAGE 51	THIS TIME - (THE ADDICTS PRAYER)
PAGE 53	I JUST WANTED TO STEAL A CAR
PAGE 55	MY DOG
PAGE 56	SHE DIDN'T HAVE TO DO IT

PAGE 58   HOW MUCH I MISS YOU MOTHER
PAGE 60   THIS PICTURE
PAGE 61   A ROSE FOR MOTHER
PAGE 62   I HAVE GOT TO GET A LIFE
PAGE 63   TIME OUT
PAGE 65   COULD THIS BE LOVE?
PAGE 66   I'M IN LOVE WITH YOU
PAGE 68   I REMEMBER
PAGE 69   WHEN YOU ARE ON MY MIND
PAGE 71   SWEETHEART
PAGE 72   I MISS YOU SO MUCH
PAGE 73   SISTA SARAH
PAGE 75   I CAN'T LET MY BLACK HOLD ME BACK
PAGE 76   YO! BRO. LIFE IS A TRIP
PAGE 79   MICKEY D THANKSGIVING
PAGE 81   IT'S CHRISTMAS TIME AGAIN
PAGE 83   HE DIDN'T HAVE TO DO IT
PAGE 84   THESE DAYS
PAGE 86   "YOU KNOW WHAT THEY SAY"
PAGE 88   CAN I HAVE MY DEMOCRACY BACK?
PAGE 94   I'M IN LOVE WITH YOU AMERICA
PAGE 98   YES YOU CAN
PAGE 100   I KNOW MY SAVIOR LIVES
PAGE 103   ST. LOUIS
PAGE 104   GOOD MORNING MR. PRESIDENT
PAGE 107   YOU HURT ME

ACKNOWLEDGMENTS

I give thanks first, to Jesus Christ, the author and finisher of my faith. Any and all benefits reaped as a result of this book are to the honor and glory of his name.

To my mother Ora Hughes, Cherry; who has gone on to her reward but who gave her five children a legacy of love, hope, dignity, charity, and respect. She instilled in us, the thirst for knowledge, the quest for truth, and the courage and ability to stand up for what is right, regardless of the foes against you. She was by far the greatest mother in the world.

To my loving family who has always been there with me in all of my endeavors, my struggles, and my triumphs. Especially to my sister, Marian Williams who always pushed me to pursue my dreams. Often saying, "With all of your talent you should be rich." Thank You Marian, for your organizational gift, your faith in me, and for always, always… being there. To my Daughter, Venise Tonette Hughes, who always says, "Dad you should write a book"

To my loving cousin Fannie Drain, who also encouraged me to write this book and, who tirelessly monitors the Henson Family web site where my music and poems were first displayed. I must thank the Henson Family members for letting me share my music and poetry on "My Family.Com." Your Comments and acceptance were invaluable.

I am eternally grateful to Terri Moore for her excellent cover design. A very special thank you, to my wonderful

Daughter-In-Law Darleen Williams, who gave me the inspiration to finally get to work on writing this book, and without whose help and patience, this book wouldn't have happened.

After publishing her own first book, "Crystal Conscience" (Available on Amazon.com) which was released March 18, 2014, Darleen urged me to publish this book of poetry which we have worked on together almost daily, from start to finish. Darleen you made it all possible. As we always, say in our partings, "I Love You"

MELVIN HUGHES

KNOWLEDGE IS POWER

To Get To The Place Where You Want To Be;
They Say You've Got To Work Harder.

I Say....To Get Where You Want To Go,
What You Have To Do Is Work Smarter.

Take The Load Off Your Back.
Your Grandpa Did That.
Did You Hear What I Said,
It's All In Your Head.

Every Day, Every Hour,
You've Got The Power,
And, Can't Nobody Stop You, But You.
Take A Look At Yourself, Not Somebody Else.
And You Do What You Know You Can Do.

Knowledge Is Power, Believe It, It's True.
Are You Listening To What I'm Saying?
The More You Know, The Farther You Can Go.
It's The Knowledge That Keep People Paying.

The Team Called Fubu,
Knew What They Could Do.
And What They Knew,
Made Them Millions.

You Know How To Do, What You,
Know How To Do, So You Could
Even Make Zillions.

If You Don't Have The Knowledge,
Find Out Where To Get It.
It's Out There For You,
You Just Haven't Met It.

You Want Some Power…. Get Some Smarts.
Keep Pushing And Don't You Dare Stop.
Fill Your Head With Things That I've Said,
That Knowledge Gets You To The Top.

Author Melvin Hughes
Copyright © 2/10/2006

YOU ARE VERY SPECIAL

You Are Very Special,
Especially You... And You.
Yes; You Are Very Special,
In Everything You Do.

You Wonder ... "What Makes
Me So Special?" "What Did I Ever Do?"
Your Uniqueness Makes You Special,
For There's No One Else Like You.

A Twin Sister, Or A Brother,
Is Born With Different Traits.
Though, They May Be Identical,
They Each Have Different Fates.

Though God Has Given Each A Gift,
No Two Gifts Are The Same.
The Gifts He Gave To Each Of Them,
Are As Different As Their Names.

It Doesn't Make You Special,
Because You're Black Or White.
The Specialty, That You Possess
Is Blind It Has No Sight.

You've Got That Special Something,
That You Must Give The World.
That Special Dream, Deep Down Inside,
Each Little Boy And Girl.

So Practice Doing What You Do Best,
And Make It Your Life's Goal.

That Special Gift That God Gave You,
Can Bring You Wealth Untold.

That Special Something That You Have,
That No One Knows About,
Will Only Be A Big Blank Space,
Until You Bring It Out.

Yes, You Are Very Special,
Believe It Cause It's True
For God Made No One Else On Earth,
The Same Way He Made You.

The Special Gift That God Gave You,
That He Gave To No One Else;
Can Only Be A Reality,
When You Believe In Yourself.

Author Melvin Hughes
Copyright © 02/09/2006

YOUR PLACE IN THE RACE

Can You Sing? Can You Dance?
Can You Cook, Or Write A Book?
Is Your Talent For Sewing
Or Long Distance Throwing?
Then You've Got A Place In The Race.

Do You Want To Fly A Plane,
Or Forecast The Rain.
Is Architecture Your Thing?
You Beautiful King.
Oh Yes! You've Got A Place In The Race.

If They Say You Can't Do It,
You Just Keep Sticking To It.
You're The Queen Of The Nile,
You're An Ebony Doll.
Girl; You've Got A Place In The Race.

No One Controls You.
I Don't Care What They Told You.
Be It Doctor, Lawyer Or Indian Chief
Whatever It Is, Be The Best You Can Be.
You've Got A Place In The Race.

Don't You Drop Out, Top Out,
Flop Out Or Cop Out.
Don't Lose Your Place In The Race.

If It Can Be Done,
Why Can't You Be The One?
What God Has For You Is For You.
God Gave You A Place In The Race.

You See... That's All Life Is
Just One Big Race…..
(I Think They Call It The Human Race)
You Should Take Your Place In The Race.

Author Melvin Hughes
Copyright © 1/22/06

TEMPER

A Temper Is A Terrible Thing,
It Causes Grief And Pain.
The Man Who Can Control It,
Is The One Who's Got The Brain.

A Temper Only Hurts You,
Each Time That You Misuse It.
Just Think What It Can Cost You,
Every Time You Lose It.

So If You Can Control It,
Surly You Will See.
When You Control Your Temper,
The Happier You Will Be.

Author Melvin Hughes
Copyright © 11/27/05

BE TRUE TO YOU

Do You Know The Heights You Can Reach?
Have You Set Your Goals To Low?
Are The Stars The Heights That You Seek?
Do You Know Where You Can Go?

Are The Preparations, You Have Made,
Enough To Get You There?
Will The Seeds That You Have Sowed Today,
Get You Up That Golden Stair?

Have You Doubt In Mind, About Your Worth?
Is Your Value Far Too Small?
Can You Stand Up Tall Against The World,
When Success In Life Has Called?

You Can't Be Somebody Else You Know,
So Don't You Even Try.
The Person You Must Be In Life
Must Be A Different Guy.

Be Better Than Your Idol,
Excel In All You Do.
Whatever Future You Have Planned,
You Must Be True To You.

Author Melvin Hughes
Copyright © 6/10/06

JUMP, BABY JUMP

Jump, Baby Jump,
You Jump Real High.
Don't You Let Nobody Tell You,
That You Can't Touch The Sky.

Even The Sky Is Not The Limit,
To What You Can Achieve.
My Child; You Can Do Anything
As Long As You Believe.

Don't Set Your Sights On Dry Land,
Let Heaven Be Your Goal,
Don't Think You Can't Do Awesome Things
Because, That's What You're Told.

I Know All Things Are Possible,
If You Have a little Faith.
So You Just Jump….. Baby Jump…….
You Jump Now Don't You Wait.

Author Melvin Hughes
Copyright © 10/27/05

ANGELS WATCHING

I Have Heard Of Angels Watching,
Keeping Watch By Day And Night.

I Have Heard They Know My Thinking.
I Have Heard They Know My Plight.

I Have Heard They Know My Secrets;
My Desires, And My Dreams.

I Have Heard That Angels Watching,
Are Aware Of Everything.

I Know The Angels Watching
To Keep Me Free From Care,

Are Sent By God The Father
So His Goodness I Can Share.

Take Care In All You Say Each Day,
Take Care In All You Do.

For God Has Sent His Angels
Who Are Always Watching You.

Perhaps There Is Some Soul That's Lost,
That Just Your Voice Can Touch.

Perhaps You Are That Angel,
That's Needed Oh So Much.

A Simple Word From You,
Could Be The Angel Sound.

Are You The Angel Watching
That The Master Has Sent Down?

Author Melvin Hughes
Copyright © 03/24/2014

I'M A SOLDIER

Lord, You Know That I'm A Soldier
And I'm Fighting In A War.
It's A War Not Of My Choosing,
In A Land That Is So Far.

I Wish That I Was Some Place Else,
Far Away From Here.
But I'm Fighting For The Freedom
That My Country Holds So Dear.

Now I Know Whatever Happens,
that Your Will Shall Be Done.
In The Twinkling Of Your Powerful
Eye, This Conflict Will Be Gone.

I Put My Trust In You Oh Lord,
And In Your Master Plan.
I Know You Are A Solid Rock
And On You, I Can Stand.

I Pray Lord That Your Blessings,
Will Be On Me This Day.
You See, Lord I'm A Soldier
In This Land So Far Away.

So I'll Just Keep On Fighting,
With The Battle In Your Hand.
Cause, You See I'm Just A Soldier,
And I'll Do The Best I Can.

Lord, You Know That I'll Keep Praying,
And When The Battle Gets To Hard.
I'll Remember That I'm A Soldier
In The Army Of The Lord.

But, If By Your will I Parish,
In This Desert Where I Roam.
I Pray That You'll Have Mercy Lord,
And Take My Spirit Home.

Author Melvin Hughes
Copyright © 8/21/05

IF JESUS CAME TODAY

If You Knew The Lord Was Coming Today
Tell Me, Just What Would You Do?
Would You Have Your House In Order,
If He Were Going To Stay With You?

Would You See That There Was Food
enough that was fit to serve A King?
Would You Open Up The Door for Him,
Or Just Let The Doorbell Ring?

Would You Pull Out Your Finest Linen,
For The Bed Where He Would Sleep?
The Vows You Made To Serve Him,
Would You Now Begin To Keep?

Would You Help One On The Corner,
That You'd Been Passing By?
Would You Help A Stranger In Need,
Or Would You Just Let Him Die?

Could You Share Some Of The Bible,
And Talk Of Things That He Had Done?
Could You Quote A Chapter And A Verse?
Could You Name A Single One?

Oh, You Know That He Is Coming;
But You Surely Don't Know When.
Will Your Life Be Filled With Jesus' Blood
Or Just Be Filled With Sin?

If You Knew That Christ Would Come
Today To Take You To Your Rest,
Would You Strive For Good Behavior,
Would You Strive To Be Your Best?

No Man Knows, When Christ Will Come,
We Don't Know When He'll Pass This Way.
Are You Sure That You'd Be Ready For Him,
If Jesus Came Today.

Author Melvin Hughes
Copyright © 09/27/2005

WHEN I WAS THERE

There Was Peace And Joy,
And yet, There Was Sadness, Most Hidden,
By The Love Of One To Another.
When I Was There.

There Was Laughter That Echoed
Through Halls, And Tears,
That Knew Not The Pain,
Of A Thousand Years,
But Of One, And That Even Shared
When I Was There.

There Was A Tastelessness,
Made Sweet, By The Kindness
Of Souls All Too Eager To Love.

There Was No Thought, Of What
Soon Would Be Returned.
When I Was There.

There Were Many Who Felt
As I Did, That, Love Can Make
All Things Good And New.
When I Was There.

And Yet, There Were Those Who Sort Not,
To Be As One With Man And God
But For Even Those I Cared........
When I Was There.

But I Fear That All These Things
Too Soon May Change, When I Have
Gone_____ So That I Must Hold On,
To The Way Things Were_____
When I Was There.

But If Joy Should Ever Leave This Place,
Let This Place Not Be Destroyed,
So I May Come Again,
And have It Be As When_____
I Was There.

Author Melvin Hughes
Copyright © 6/14/1993

IF I SHOULD DIE, BEFORE I WAKE

I Want To Do The Best I Can,
With This Life That God Gave Me.
I Want To Be A Shining Light,
    For Every One To See.

I Want To Help My Fellow Man,
    And Give Each One A Helping Hand.
I Hope I've Lived The Masters Plan,
    If I Should Die, Before I Wake.

I Hope That I Have Lived A Life,
    That's Shown Someone The Way.
I Hope I've Found A Lamb That's Lost
    And Gave Him Hope Today.

Did I Help To Heal A Broken Heart,
    Help Fix A Life That's Torn Apart.
I hope I Gave You Strength To Make A Start,
    If I Should Die, Before I Wake.

If Words That I Uttered,
Brings Peace While In The Storm,
If I Have Taught Some Child I Saw,
The Right Before The Wrong.

I Hope That I Gave Love,
To Someone In Despair,
I Hope I Gave A Smile One Day,
To Show Someone I Care.

I Hope That I Have Helped Someone,
Just For Goodness Sake.
I Pray My Life Was Not In Vain,
If I Should Die Before I Wake.

Author: Melvin Hughes
Copyright © 09/30/2005

WHERE IS YOUR FAITH ?

I Hear You Say You Trust The Lord.
Now, If That's Really True.
Then Why Is There So Little Faith,
In Everything You Do?

You Kneel Down At The Alter,
Your Mind So Full Of Doubt,
Your Heart Just Not Believing,
That God Will Work It Out.
He's Always, Been There For You,
Time, And Time Again,
But You Are Not So Sure
This Time, The Savior Will Step In.

OH! Ye Of Little Faith,
I Say To You Today.
If You Are Going To Worry,
Why Take The Time To Pray?

Didn't He Save You Yesterday?
Then, Today He'll Bring You Out.
So If You're Taking Time to Pray
What Are You Worried About?
Author Melvin Hughes
Copyright © 10/07/2005

IF YOUR CROSS IS TOO HEAVY…
CARRY MINE
(ORIGINAL POEM TAKEN
FROM A STORY (Author Unknown)

I Went To God In Prayer One Day,
About The Cross I Had To Bear.

So He Took Me Into A Great Big Room,
And There Were Many Crosses There.

Well, I Looked The Crosses Over,
And Began To Try Them On.

The First Was Much Too Heavy,
So I Tried Another One.

Most Of Them Were Heavy,
Or Too Tattered And Beat Up,

Some Of Them Were Blood Stained
Like The Master's Bitter Cup.

Cross After Cross, All Day Long,
I Put Upon My Back,

I Refused To Give Up Trying,
Until; I Found One That I Like.

So, I Told Him; I'll Take This One,
It's Really Light And Thin.

He Said…………..
"Are You Sure This Is The Cross You Want?"
" It's The One You Just Brought In "

Author Melvin Hughes
Copyright © 06/20/2005

THANK YOU

I Took A Breath, Then I Took Two,
Then God Let Me Take Three.

Then I Said, Father I Thank You,
For The Breath Inside Of Me.

Father, I Thank You For These Hands,
That Let Me Do Thy Work.

Thank You For The Feet You Gave
To Walk Upon This Earth.

I Thank You For These Eyes To See,
And For A Tongue To Speak.

I Thank You For This Brain Of Mine,
So Knowledge I May Seek.

I Thank You For The Sunshine.
I Thank You For The Rain.

Father, I Just Say, Thank You,
For Being My Everything.

With Ten Thousand Tongues I Couldn't Say,
Thank You Enough For All You Do Each Day.

Lord.... Because Of Who You Are............
I Just Say Thank You!

Author Melvin Hughes
Copyright © 08/15/2005

THE ANGEL VOICE

There's An Angel Who Was Singing,
In A Voice Both Loud And Clear.
There's An Angel That Was Singing,
Who Was Never Hard To Hear.

There Were Some Who Were Annoyed;
For His Voice Was Not That Great.
But He Sung The Hymns Of Gospel,
In A Voice That Could Not Wait.

Oh, The Choir Wished Him Silent,
For His Voice Just Did Not Blend.
It Was Way Off Key And Shaky,
And Everybody Stared At Him.

How He Sang The Songs Of Zion,
And He Followed Every Line.
He Was Singing Every Sunday,
And Was Always There On Time.

Then One Day The Congregation Sang,
But Listened With Dismay,
For The Pew That Held The Angel Voice
Had Nothing More To Say.

You See, God Awakened Him This Morning,
With A Brand New Song To Sing.
And There Was No Organ Playing,
Just A Peaceful Joy Bell Ring.

So, We Ought Not Be Complaining,
Of A Voice That Does Not Mix,
For It Just Might Be An Angel Voice,
That Only God Can Fix.

Oh; The Choir; well they're Still Singing,
But The Song Just Seems All Wrong.
It Just Seems There's Something Missing,
Since The Angel Voice Is Gone.

He Was Singing Not For Show,
Nor For Pleasure Did He Sing.
He Was Singing Giving Glory,
To His Master, Lord, And King.

While We All Wished, He'd Be Quiet,
He Was Sending Up His Prayer.
He Was Tuning Up That Angel Voice
So He Could Sing With Heaven's Choir.

Author Melvin Hughes
Copyright© 5/22/2005

I TOLD MY FRIEND TO PRAY

A Friend Of Mine Came To Me One Day,
He Was Very Troubled In Mind.

I Said I Could Offer A Little Advice,
And He Thought Was Very Kind.

I Said; "Why Not Be More Respectful,
And Walk In A Better Way"

But I Think Words That Helped The Most
Was, I Told My Friend To Pray.

He Looked At Me Rather Strangely,
As If Not To Understand.

I Looked At Him In Earnestness
As If His Life Was At Hand.

I Explained the Meaning of Prayer,
And Told Him Why, He Should Pray.

At First, He Listened In Anger,
Then Heard What I Had To Say.

It Seems To Me, Such A Pity,
That Christians Let Sinners Stray.

All It Takes And The Difference It Makes,
To Just Tell A Friend To Pray.

God Knows About Your Situation,
He's Waiting To Save You Today.

He Will Give You Salvation, If You
Fall On Your Knees And You Pray

Author Melvin Hughes
Copyright © 08/25/05

I LOST MY FRIEND TODAY

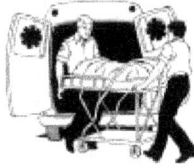

I Lost A Friend Not To Long Found,
I Had Her But A Year.

In That Time, This Friend Of Mine
Was Someone Very Dear.

I'm Not Alone Since She Has Gone
Though, At Times Is Seems That Way.

I Know She's With Me Even Now
But I Lost My Friend Today.

Kind... That Puts It Mildly.
Good... Is So Little To Say.

She, Was So Much More Than That
To Me But, I Lost My Friend Today.

I Wanted To Keep Her With Me,
Though I Knew, She Could Not Stay.

God Knew Her Pain And Suffering……..
So He Took My Friend Today.

Author Melvin Hughes
Copyright © 05/15/2005

DON'T FORGET TO PRAY

When You Got Up This Morning
And You Breathed In Clean, Fresh Air.

Did You Thank The Lord For Blessings
that He Already Had Put There?

Did You Thank Him For His Keeping
As You Slept The Night Away?

Did You Ask If He Would Guide You
As You go About Your Day?

Did You Ask If He Would Bless You,
And Keep You Safe From Harm?

Do You Just Take Him For Granted
As You Travel Through The Storm?

Just Remember At The End Of Things,
The Debt That You Must Pay,

Will Be So Much Less Expensive
If You Don't Forget To Pray.

Author Melvin Hughes
Copyright © 08/12/2005

EVERY DAY AIN'T PRETTY

Some Days You Really Hate To Get Up,
It Turns Out To Be Your Best Day.
Some Days You Get Up Running,
And Nothing Goes Your Way.

You Know.....Every Day Ain't Pretty.

The Sun Will Shine Some Days,
Then Other Days It Rains.
Some Days You Feel Like A Million
Others You're Filled With Pain.

Nope.....Every Day Ain't Pretty

But Even Days When You Feel Sad,
Thank God, At Least You're Feeling.
And Even Days When Feeling Bad,
The Scrapes And Scratches Are Healing.

Well...Every Day Ain't Pretty,
But By The Grace Of God...
It Is, Another Day.

Author Melvin Hughes
Copyright © 10/28/05

KATRINA

Katrina, What Have You Done To Me?
Girl, What Have You Done?
You Took The Only Place I Knew,
The Place That I Called Home.

You've Uprooted My Family.
You've Taken Us Far Away.
We Don't Know What Is Happening,
As We Go From Day To Day.

One Day We're Here In Houston
The Next In San Antone
Town To Town, Day To Day,
Trying To Find A Home.

I Hope The World Did Not Forget,
All That We Went Through.
I Hope Someone Is Watching,
Everything We Do.

I'm Sure That We Will Be All Right,
It's Just Going To Take Some Time.
With Prayers And Help From God Above,
I'm Sure We'll Be Just Fine.

But Don't You All Forget Us,
Don't Let Us Go Astray.
Just Keep On Praying And Saying
God, Keep Them Just One More Day.

Author Melvin Hughes
Copyright © 11/15/02005

LET'S HAVE ANOTHER
HONEYMOON

I Can't Hear You. I'm Talking.
We're Out Of Step.
You're Running. I'm Walking.

My Day Is Your Night.
We're Not Together.
Your Wrong Is My Right.

Your New Is My Old.
Is There Common Ground?
My Hot Is Your Cold.

I Said I Do.
What Ever Happen To "US" ?
You Said It Too.

"The Great Big I And Little Bitty You"
when people Are Married, That Just Won't Do.

It's Time To Rediscover
Why We Really Love Each Other.

Tell Me, Why Can't We Communicate,
And Find That Place Where Love Waits?

Why Don't You And I Go There Soon.
Let's Have Another Honeymoon.

Author Melvin Hughes
Copyright © 06/15/05

HAPPY BIRTHDAY

I THINK SOMEONE SHOULD TELL YOU,
I THING SOMEONE SHOULD SAY.
YOU GO HAVE ALL THE FUN YOU WANT,
AFTER ALL, IT'S YOUR BIRTHDAY.

JUST HAVE YOURSELF A PARTY.
KICK OFF YOUR SHOES AND STUFF,
CAUSE ALL THE FUN THAT YOU CAN HAVE,
CAN NEVER BE ENOUGH.

SO I SAY.... GO... PLAY.....
DO WHATEVER YOU WANT,
AND DO IT YOUR WAY.

WHATEVER YOU DECIDE TO DO,
I SAY HAPPY BIRTHDAY TO YOU.

AUTHOR MELVIN HUGHES
COPYRIGHT © 10/22/05

THE FAMILY REUNION

I Went To The Family Reunion,
Not Knowing Who I'd Meet....

I Tell You Before I Left There
I Was Swept Right Off My Feet.

I Laughed, I Cried, I Danced,
And I Prayed; All In Just Three Days.

I Met New Kin From Everywhere.....
I Tell You I Was Truly Amazed.

I Haven't Seen Such Real True Love,
Since I Can't Tell You When.

In Fact... I Enjoyed Myself So Much
That I'm Going Back Again.

Author Melvin Hughes
Copyright © 6/10/2000

THE THINGS I NEVER SAID

You Left So Suddenly It Seems,
There Wasn't Time To Say,
So Many Things, That were
Left Unsaid, That Very Final Day.

You Were The Angel In My Life,
The Star That Shined So Bright.
Darling, You Were All That I Lived For…..
You Made My Whole World Right.

How I Loved You, And Adored You,
And I Should Have Told You So.
I Didn't Say A Lot Of Things,
That I Wanted You To Know.

I Should Have Told You Everything,
Before God Took You Home.
But Time Would Not Stand Still For Me
And, Now My Love You're Gone.

It's Funny, Since You Left Me,
The Things Inside My Head.
My Mind Just Keeps Repeating,
All The Things I Never Said.

Author Melvin Hughes
Copyright © 09/28/2005

TOMORROW MIGHT BE TOO LATE

Have You Told Someone,
"I Love You" Today?
Did You Think, "Oh, It Can Wait"
You Should Say It Now To Someone.
Tomorrow Might Be Too Late.

That Fight You Had Was So Trivial.
Why Did It Breed So Much Hate?
Move On, My Friend, Forget It.
Tomorrow Might Be Too Late.

Best Wishes And Flowers,
And Kisses For Hours,

Remember That Very First Date.
Remember, What It Was Like Before,
Tomorrow Might Be Too Late.

How Long Will You Be Here?
Are You Sure About Your Fate?
Take Time Today.
Heal The Wounds You've Made.
Tomorrow Might Be Too Late.

Author Melvin Hughes
Copyright © 10/24/05

I'M SORRY

At Times Words Can Not Reveal,
Exactly, What My Heart May Feel.

Simple Words Meant To Heal,
Wounds Misspoken Words Conceal.

Sometime I Simply Need To Say,
I'm Sorry Things Turned Out That Way.

I Need To Say;
I Love You And I'm Sorry.

Author Melvin Hughes
Copyright © 10/12/2005

ME AND MY FRIEND GIN

I'm Sitin' In This Bar, Drinking All Alone,

Thinkin' To Myself, You Outta Be Home.

But I Know If I Go Home, I Can't Get In.
So, I'm Staying With My Friend, Gin.

I Have Lost My Job, And Wrecked The Car,
So I Ended Up Here In This Stinkin' Bar.

For The Life Of Me I Just Can't Win,
And It's Because Of My Friend, Gin.

I Tried To Get Straight.
I Guess I'll Have To Try Harder.
Because These Lies I Keep Tellin'
They Just Don't Hold Water.

Maybe Someday, I'll Get It Right,
Put Down My Gloves...Give Up The Fight,
But, As You Can See, I'm Drunk Again.
Me And My Friend, Gin.
As For Today My Friend,.....

It's Just Me And My Friend, Gin.
Author Melvin Hughes
Copyright © 10/21/2005

THIS TIME
(THE ADDICTS PRAYER)

I've Got To Make Some Changes,
In The Way I Live My Life.
I Have Got To Make Some Changes.
I've Got To Get It Right.
This Time

I Know I Said The Last Time,
"I've Got It All Together"
I Told Myself And Others,
I Was Off This Stuff Forever.
It'll Be Different.
This Time

I Beg You Lord To Listen.
Hear My Humble Prayer.
I Need Your Help Dear Lord.
I Need You To Be There.
This Time

Lord, Deliver Me From Myself.
Please, Help Me As I Try.
Without Your Help..... This Time......
I Know That I Will Die.
This Time

51

I Know You've Heard It All Before.
You've Heard It, And You've Seen It.
I Am Going To Change My Life Today.
This Time..... I Really Mean It!

Author Melvin Hughes
Copyright © 10/20/05

I JUST WANTED TO STEAL A CAR

All That I Did Was Steal A Car.
I Didn't Want To Keep It, Or Drive It To Far.
I Had To Drive It Fast, Couldn't Drive It Slow
I Had To See How Fast, This Baby Would Go.
I Just Wanted To Steal A Car.

I Had To Show My Homies, That I Could Do It.
They Already Told Me, "Ain't Nothing To It".
Didn't Give No Thought, To The Cost.
That Somebody's Life Could Be Lost.
I Just Wanted To Steal A Car.

The Cops Gave Chase And The Race Was On.
I Hit Some Cars But I Kept On Going.
Then I Hit Somebody, But I Didn't Stop.
Later On They Told Me, I Had Killed A Cop.
I Just Wanted To Steal A Car.

The Time They Gave Me, Can't Wipe Away,
The Pain And The Hurt That I Feel Today.

Listening To My Homie's, Didn't Get Me Far.
It's Far Much More Than Just Stealing A Car.

They Gave Me Life, Then, They Gave More.
I Just Can't Figure Out, What I Did That For.

All I Think About Behind These Bars.......
I Just Wanted To Steal A Car.

Author Melvin Hughes
Copyright © 1/24/2006

MY DOG

HE'S ALWAYS THERE WHEN I COME HOME,
HE NEVER COMPLAINS ABOUT BEING ALONE.

HE'S VERY OBEDIENT AND HE DOESN'T TALK BACK
AND, OF SPECIAL LOVE THERE IS NO LACK.
HE JUST EATS AND SLEEPS..... BARKS SOMETIME,
DOESN'T ASK FOR A NICKEL, OR A DIME.

DOESN'T GET UPSET AND RANT OR POUT,
HE EVEN LETS ME KNOW WHEN HE WANTS OUT.

DON'T ASK FOR NOTHING BUT LOVE AND CARE,
JUST WANTS TO KNOW THAT SOMEONE'S THERE.

YEP!!!

THAT'S MY COMPANION UNTIL THE END,
HE'S MY BABY....."MY DOG"..... MY FRIEND....

AUTHOR MELVIN HUGHES
COPYRIGHT © 10/31/05

SHE DIDN'T HAVE TO DO IT
BUT SHE DID

She Carried Me Inside Her Body,
And Endured The Pain Of Childbirth.

She Raised Me from A little Child,
And Instilled In Me Self Worth.

She Kept Me Warm And Kept Me Dry,
And Pick Me Up Each Time I'd Cry.
She Really Didn't Have To Do It,
But She Did.

She Scared The Boogieman For Me,
When I Couldn't Sleep At Night.

She Filled Me With Great Values And
How To tell What's Wrong Or Right.

She Didn't Have To Wipe My Teardrops,
And Shelter Me From Raindrops.
She Really Didn't Have To Do It,
But She Did.

She Didn't Have To Fix My Meals
For Me, Each Morning, Noon, And Night,

She Healed My Cuts And Scrapes A Lot,
Each Time That I Would Fight,

She Didn't Have To Kiss And Hug Me,
Just To Show How Much She Loved Me.
She Didn't Have Pray For Me,
But She Did.

Mom Took Me To Sunday School.
She Told Me That Loving God Was Cool.

She Didn't Have To Do, A Lot Of Things,
Like Teach Me To Believe In Dreams.

She Taught Me To Respect Myself,
And Have Respect For everyone Else.

Tell Me Just Where Would I Be,
My Lord …...Can You Tell Me?

If It Had Not Been For All The Things…
That Mother Did.

Author Melvin Hughes
Copyrighted © 5/8/2005

57

HOW MUCH I MISS YOU MOTHER

Sometimes I Didn't Show You.
Sometimes I Never Told You,
But You Were Really Golden.
How Much I Miss You Mother.

What I Miss So Much,
Is Your Sweet Voice, And Gentle Touch,
Your Words Of Wit And Wisdom.
Oh, How Much I Miss You Mother.

There Is None Like You.
Who Could Do The Things You Do?
You Were Some Kind Of Magician.
How Much I Miss You Mother.

I Thought You'd Never Leave Me,
Now You're Gone, How It Grieves Me.
But You Are Always There It Seems.
How Much I Miss You Mother.

Looking Back Over Your Life,
Your Trouble And Your Strife.
Your Dignity And Your Grace,
Made Such A Special Place.

It Makes Me Know Just Why,
"How Much I Miss You Mother"

Author Melvin Hughes
Copyright © 5/6/2006

THIS PICTURE

I've Got This Perfect Picture Of You,
It's With Me All The Time.
Now No One Sees This Picture,
Because It's Personal And It's Mine.

If I don't See You In Person,
You'll Still Be There It Seems.
Because, Although You're Not In Person,
You're Still There In My Dreams.

In This Picture, I Can See,
Such A Pretty Face.
This Picture Will Be In My Head,
Until My Dying Day.

Author Melvin Hughes
Copyright © 12/07/05

A ROSE FOR MOTHER

Here's A Rose For Mother,
That's Truly Meant To Say.

How Sad We Were And How We Grieved,
The Day That You Went Away.

It's Meant To Say We Thank You,
For The Love And Care You Gave.

We Thank You For The Sacrifices,
That We All Know You Made.

It's Meant To Say We Miss You Still,
Even Though You've Gone Away.

And We Await That Glorious Morning
When We'll Meet Again Some Day.

Author Melvin Hughes

I HAVE GOT TO GET A LIFE

I Certainly Am Not Old Yet,
But I'm Getting Older Every Day.

I Got To Change The Way I Live,
I Can't Go On This Way.

Can't Be Afraid To Love Again,
Cause I've Been Hurt Before.

I'm Sure There Is A Love For Me,
To Cherish And Adore.

Don't Know, If I'll Make That Step Again;
Being Somebody's Wife.

But One Thing That I Do Know Is...

<u>I Have Got To Get A Life.</u>

Author Melvin Hughes
Copyright © 10/10/2005

TIME OUT

Women, Can You Tell Me,
How Do You Define Your Man?
Is He Just Another Paycheck?
Or Is He Wonderful, And Grand?

Is He Someone You Can Count On,
When The Chips Are Down?
Do You Think That He's Just Someone,
Kind Of Nice To Have Around?

Men, What About Your Woman,
Is She Everything You Need?
Is She Worth Her Weight In Gold To You?
Is She Your Best Friend Indeed?

Is She Comfort When You're Lonely,
And Joy When You Feel Down?
Do You Think That She's Just Someone
Kind Of Nice To Have Around?

Do You Take Each Other For Granted,
Thinking All Is Going Fine?
Have You Learned Yet To Communicate,
And Have Some Quiet Time?

Do You Have Faith And Trust,
And Little Room To Doubt?
Are There Problems And Concerns…
That You Need To Talk About?

Get A Handle On The Problem,
Discuss What It's About.
Are You The One, Who's Always Right?
Take Time To Work It Out.

If Everything Is Going Well
And Your Relationship Is Fine.
You've Got The Love That's Sure To Last,
And Stand The Test Of Time.

Make A Date For Dinner, And A Dance,
And Get A Sitter For The Kids.
Take Time Out… Enjoy Each Other…..
You'll Be Awfully Glad You Did.

Author Melvin Hughes
Copyright © 3/2/2006

COULD THIS BE LOVE?

Before You, There Was Darkness.
The Sun, Never Seemed To Shine.
I Was Always Feeling Lonely,
Deep Down In This Heart Of Mine.

It Seemed The World Had Been Unfair,
And Hadn't Given Me My Due.
Then One Day, As Though From A Dream,
There In My World Was You.

Had My Prayers Of Years Been Answered?
Had The Gods Now Smiled On Me?
Had My Knight In Shining Armor,
Finally Come To Set Me Free?

Because Now My Whole World Sparkles,
Brighter Than The Stars Above.
I Think.... My God.... What Is This Miracle?
Could It Be That This Is Love?

Author Melvin Hughes
Copyright © 11/13/05

I'M IN LOVE WITH YOU

You Ask Me Why I Love You,
I Don't Know Why I Do.

All That I Know, That I Know, I Know Is,
I'm In Love With You.

My Head Says I Should Wait A While,
It Says, "Don't Get In To Deep"

My Heart Won't Listen To My Head,
It Wants To Take That Leap.

You Say, "How Do You Know Love?"
"How Can You Be So Sure?"

I Know I Had This Heartache,
That Only You Could Cure.

How Do I Know That I Love You,
How Can I Show No Fear?

My Head Asks All The Questions,
My Heart Doesn't Want To Hear.

There's Something About The Way
I Feel, Each Time I See Your Face.

I Want To Kiss And Hug You,
And Touch You Every Place.

I Know I Want You With
Me, Everywhere I Go.

I Want To Shout From Mountaintops
I Want The World To Know.

How Do I Know I Love You,
It's In The Way You Talk

The Way You Dress, And Wear Your Hair;
Your Smile, Your Style, Your Walk.

I Don't Care, Why I Love You,
I Only Know I Do.

The Only Thing That Matters
To Me Is... I'm In Love With You.

Author Melvin Hughes
Copyright © 09/22/2005

I REMEMBER

I Remember The Beauty Of The Ocean.
I Remember The Look In Your Eyes.

I Remember The Beauty Of The Sunset Too
As It Covered The Evening Sky.

I Remember How Happy That Made You,
Happier Than You've Ever Been.

I Remember Thinking, How Lucky I Am
To Have You, As My Friend.

Author Melvin Hughes
Copyright © 9/18/05

WHEN YOU ARE ON MY MIND

I Think Of Lot's Of Things At Times.
There's Fall And Spring And Birds That Sing.
When You Are On My Mind.

There're Rivers Flowing To The Sea, And
The Breeze Of A Midsummer Night's Dream,
When You Are On My Mind.

The Beat Of The Drum In A Big Parade, And
A Heart That Seems To March To That Beat.
When You Are On My Mind.

There's A Snow Capped Mountain,
Where Skiers Ski. I Think Of You,
Then I Think Of Me.

My Mind Wonders…. And Yet In That
Wondering, The Thought Of You Lingers.
When You Are On My Mind.

I Have Visions Of A Kiss,
A Kiss That Only You Could Give.
When You Are On My Mind.

The Kiss You Gave Caused My Heart
To Sing, And It Took My Breath Away.
Still You're On My Mind.

The Passion Builds Within Me,
For The Longing Of Your Arms,
When You Are On My Mind.

I Hear The Comfort Of Your Sweet Words,
The Words That Soothe My Very Soul,
Saying, All Is Right With The World.

The Day Ends, And Our Love Blends,
And I Am At Peace……………
When You Are On My Mind.

Author Melvin Hughes
Copyright © 05/15/22005

SWEETHEART

I WANT YOU TO KNOW
THAT I APPRECIATE YOU,
FOR ALL OF YOUR LOVE,
AND ALL THAT YOU DO.

THE GENTLE WAY THAT YOU KISS ME,
THE WARMTH THAT I FEEL INSIDE,
THE WAY YOU MAKE TOES CURL,
IS JUST TOO MUCH TO HIDE.

THE SILLY THINGS YOU SAY SOMETIME,
AND YOU KEEP ME SMILING TOO.
NO WONDER AFTER ALL THESE YEARS,
I'M STILL IN LOVE WITH YOU.

AUTHOR MELVIN HUGHES
COPYRIGHT © 10/10/05

I MISS YOU SO MUCH

I Never Knew, How Much I Loved You.
I Never Knew, How Much I Cared.
I Didn't Know How Much I'd Miss You,
Until You Weren't There.

The Sweet, Sweet Music, We Made,
I Thought Would Always Be.
I Didn't Know The Band Would Stop,
The Day That You Left Me.

I'm Sure The Music Will Be Sweet
Again, The Day That You Return.
Till That Day I'll Ponder,
All That I Have Learned.

The Doctor Says I'll Be Ok,
And All Will Be In Tact.
He Says, I'll Sing As Good As New,
As Soon As My Voice Comes Back.

Author Melvin Hughes
Copyright © 10/27/05

SISTA SARAH

Anybody Done Seen Sista Sarah,
I Don't Know Where She Gone.

The Last Time That I Saw Her,
She Was A Headin' For Her Home.

Said She Was Going To The Kitchen,
To Fix Some Apple Pie.

But I Can't Find Sista Sarah,
And I Done Looked Both Low An' High.

Have You Looked And Seen Sista Sarah,
Can't Find Her For The Life Of Me.

She Been Gone Now Most All Mornin'
I'm Get Worried Can't You See.

Is She Gone Through The Church Yard,
Done Took A Little Short Cut?

She Trying To Get Home To That Kitchen,
Where She Loves To Cook So Much.

Anybody Done Seen Siesta Sarah'
You All Know Where She Gone?

You Tell Her That I Been A Waitin'
You Tell Her I Say Come Home.

She Might Done Gone To The Apple Yard,
To Shake That O'l Apple Tree.

Sho' Hope There Ain't Nutin' Happened,
Cause She Was A Makin' That Pie For Me.

AUTHOR MELVIN HUGHES
COPYRIGHT © 09/29/2005

I CAN'T LET MY BLACK
HOLD ME BACK

"You Want To Do What?"
"You're Kidding I'm Sure."
"There Is No Way You Can Do That."

Sir... You Must Be Mistaken,
Because This Job I'm taking.
I Can't Let My Black Hold Me Back.

It's One Step At A Time.
Every Nickel And every Dime,
I'm Keeping My Life In Tack.

No Matter What You Say,
I'm Gonna Do It My Way,
I Can't Let My Black Hold Me Back.

It Takes A Whole Lot Of Learning,
And Some Twisting And Turning,
To Reach The Other Side Of The Track,

You See, I Can Do, Anything I Want To, If
I Don't Let My Black Hold Me Back.

Author Melvin Hughes
Copyright © 10/29/05

YO! BRO LIFE IS A TRIP

So I Burn The City Down, I Don't Give A Damn.
Don't Nobody Really Care About Who I Am.
Ain't Got No Job, So I Run The Streets, Cause
Ain't Nobody Out Here, Who Cares About Me.

I Mean White Folks Say,
There's Something
Wrong With My Kind.
So I Just Run Around Acting,
Like I Lost My Mind.

"YO! Bro Life Is A Trip"

Don't They Know,
I Wanna Live A Good Life.
Don't Make No Difference
If I'm Black Or White.

I Just Wanna Be Happy
Like Everybody Else.
Have A Job, A Family,
And Respect For Myself.

I Got An Education,
Job Training Too,
But There Ain't No Jobs,
So What Good Did That Do?

"YO! Bro Life Is A Trip"

So The Rich Get Richer Kickin'
Po Folks Around .
They say; "
Just Let The Money,
Keep Trickling Down."

Now They Keep Getting Richer,
Robin' All Of Us Blind.
Trying To Fight All That Money
Is A Waste Of My Time.

"YO! Bro Life Is A Trip"

The Drugs Is Killin' Brothers,
That's What They Want It To Do,
So They Can Always Keep
The Finger, Pointed Right You.

You See It's Just Another Way,
Of Keepin' You Down,
So There'll Be Less Of You
Po People Hanging Around,

YO! Bro Life Is A Trip"

You Gettin' To Much Welfare.
Talkin' Bout, Equal Rights.
It Works Better For Them,
If You Ain't Got No Life.

If You Do Get A Job, The Pay Is So Bad,
They Pay You Just Enough Money
To Keep You Hungry and Mad.

"YO! Bro Life Is A Trip"

Well, Some Of Us Will Make It,
And I Thank God For That.
It's Truly A Blessin'
They Can't Hold All Of Us Back.

Don't You Forget To Reach Back,
And Give Us A Hand.
And we'll just Keep On Fighting,
Doin' The Best That We Can.

Believe Me! Bro.!
Life Is A Trip.

Author Melvin Hughes
Copyright © 12/03/05

MICKEY D THANKSGIVING

Who's Fixing The Turkey This Year
Grandma Is It You?
Boy, Go And Ask Your Mamma
Turkey Is Something I Don't Do.

Mamma Are You Doing The Turkey
With The Cornbread Stuffing And Stuff?
Mamma You Know When You Fix Turkey,
I Just Can't Get Enough.

I'm Not Fixing Turkey Or Dressing,
Mashed Potatoes Or Black-Eyed Peas.
We're All Going Out To Dinner This Year.
We'll Be Eating At Mickey D's

But Mamma, Its Thanksgiving,
Shouldn't We Be Eating At Home?
I'm Not Cooking, And That's That,
Now You Leave Your Mamma Alone.

"I Hate To Tell Them We Can't Afford It,
But I Have To Tell Them... I Just Can't Lie.
A Few Hamburgers And Some French Fries
Is All That We Can Buy."

Thank God We've Still Got A House,
And Lord, They've Still Got Mother.

**We Don't Have A Lot Of Money,
But Thank God, Got Each Other.**

**Author Melvin Hughes
Copyright © 11/13/05**

IT'S CHRISTMAS TIME AGAIN

Now Dance With Glee
Oh My, Oh Me,
It's Christmas Time Again.

Christmas Bells Are Ringing.
Carolers Are Singing.
It's Christmas Time Again.

The Ground Is All White,
And It's Such A Pretty Sight.
It's Christmas Time Again.
Presents And Toys,
For Little Girls And Boys.
It's Christmas Time Again.

It's The Birthday Of Jesus.
He Gave Us The Reason,
For Christmas Time Again.

So Let Us Not Ignore Him.
OH! Come Let Us Adore Him.
It's Christmas Time Again.

Give Him Honor And Glory.
Remember The Story.
It's Christmas Time Again.

Give Praises To God The Father,
Who Gave To Us, His Son.

He Wrapped Them All Together,
So They All Became Just One.
Now It's Christmas Time Again.

Author Melvin Hughes
Copyright © 12/24/05

HE DIDN'T HAVE TO DO IT
BUT HE DID

The Dawn Is Breaking On A Brand New Year,
And I Thank My God That I'm Still Here.
I'm Blessed To Know That He Still Cares.
He Didn't Have To Let Me Live, But He Did.

He Didn't Have To Bless Me So Abundantly.
He Didn't Have To Do All That He Did For Me.
I Just Thank Him, For Letting Me Live,
Cause He Didn't Have To Do It But He Did.

He Spared Me To See Just One More Day,
Just One More Sunshine He Sent My Way,
With Health And Strength Enough To Say,
I Know He Didn't Have To Do It But He Did.

Someone Sweeter Than I Am
Won't Pass This Way Again.
Someone Much Better Than I Am,
Didn't See This Old Year End.

But He Loved Me Enough
To Give Me, Just A Little More Time.
He Showered Me With Blessings,
And Spared This Life Of Mine. I Know,
He Didn't Have To Do It But He Did.

Author Melvin Hughes
Copyright © 1/01/2006

THESE DAYS

These Days Are So Troubling,
We're Going Through Trying Times.
There's Trouble In This Nation;
In This Wondrous Land Of Mine.

There Seems To Be No Fairness,
No Justice, No Respect.
There Just Seems To Be All
This Discourse,
Poor Direction And Neglect.

The Price Of Things Get Higher,
While The Wages Stay The Same.
How Are We Ever, To Survive,
Tell Me, In Jesus' Name.

The Climate Keeps On Changing,
And No One Seems To Care.
There's So Much Greed And Hatred,
And Chaos Every Everywhere.

There's Just Too Many Suffering,
From The Misery Of War.
The Rich Keep Getting Richer,
While The Poor Keep Getting Poorer.

The Love Of Money Is The Root Of All Evil,
That's The Number One Reason For
All This Upheaval.

Discrimination Is Rampant.
We Can't Seem To Get Along.
It's Appalling And Petty,
But Above All Else It's Wrong.

Guns And More Guns, Are Filling The Street.
We're Just Killing Each Other, Too Blind To See.
Lord...... Help Us To Change Our Ways,
We Sure Do Need You Right Now Lord.....
Lord....We Need You Now.....
These Days

Author Melvin Hughes
Copyright © 4/23/2014

"YOU KNOW WHAT THEY SAY"

Wake Up People, Wake Up.

They Taking Your Vote Away.
The Vote That People Died For,
You Losing It Every Day.

They Say……
"They Goin' Round Here Just A Voting;
Electin' People And Stuff.
They' Getin' Too Much Power,
And We Have Had Enough".

They Say……
"They' Got So Much Power;
Now The Presidents Is Black.
Yea! They Got To Much Power
We Got To Pullum' Back".

They Say……
"We Got To Stopum,' From Votin' On Sunday,
And We Got Take The Polls Away.
We Got To Do Somethin', And Do It Fast.
They Getin' Stronger Every Day".

They Say……
"We Got To Change The Way They Votin',

And They Can't Vote Early No More.
On Votin Night Put Up A Fight.
If They Try To Get In The Door."

They Say…….
"We Need Long Lines……….
So People Get Tired; Get Mad;
And Go Home,
Cause If They Stay In This Line An' Vote,
The Vote's Gonna Turn Out Wrong".

They Say…..
"If We Keep On Letin Um' Vote,
We'll Always Lose In The End.
So, We Got To Stopum' From Votin,
Cause That's The Only Way We Can Win".

Now You Go And Tell Every Body.

Tell City And Country Folk.
Because If You Don't Tell Them,
They Won't Wake Up, And
They're Going To Lose Their Vote.

Author Melvin Hughes
Copyright © 4/23/2014

CAN I HAVE MY DEMOCRACY BACK?

Can I Please Have My Democracy Back?
I'm Getting Pretty Upset And That's A Fact.
You're Doing Your Best To Take It All Away.
You Keep Tearing It Down, Every Single Day.

I'm Getting Pretty Upset With All That.
Can You Give Me My Democracy Back?

Fat Cats, Are Buying The Senate.
They're Buying The Courts And The House.
They're Buying Every Race In The Country,
You Know What I'm Talking About.

I Can See, Just Where You Are At.
Now, Can I Have My Democracy Back?

You Don't Want Me To Vote, Cause You Can't Win.
You've Tried To Take My Vote, Again And Again.

The Lines Are Too Long. Can't Vote On Sunday,
You Trying To Make Me Go Home.
Cause I'm Working On Monday.

No Voting On Week Ends,
You Want To Change, What Has Been.

Taking Away The Polls.
You Want To Shorten The Rolls.

We Demand, That You Stop Doing That.
We Just Want Our Democracy Back?

I Guess You Just Don't Care, If Elections Are Fair,
If There's Poverty, And Misery, Everywhere

So The Rich Richer, The Poor Get Poorer.
Some Get Less, While Others Get More.

Hey! This Is The Country We Love?
You Trying To Fly With Eagles,
But You're Sleeping With Doves.

Somebody Teach These People How To Act.
They Need To Give My Democracy Back?

I Thought Justice Was Blind
But She's Got Eyes.

The Courts Are Corrupt,
And They are Filled With Lies.

Hating And Lying On The President
Won't Pass No Laws, It Don't Make Sense.

Create Some Jobs Is What
You Need To Do.

It Doesn't Matter Whether States
Are Red Or Blue.

Straighten Up And Fly Right Jack.
I Want My Democracy Back?

Some Of Us, Get Layoffs.
While Others Get Payoffs.

They're Robbing Us Blind,
And That's A Crime.

You Say You Don't Want Welfare.
But I Can't Have Health Care.

No Food Stamps... And No Equal Pay,
But Prices Keep Rising Getting Higher Each Day.

You Act Like, You're On Some Kinda Crack.
Give Me, My Democracy Back?

First Amendment Rights..........
Second Amendment Rights......
Millionaire Rights........
Billionaire Rights.......
Gun Owner Rights.........
Religious Rights...........
LGBT Rights...........
Women's Right.......
Human Rights...........
Stand Your Ground Rights........

Everybody's Got Rights Are These Rights
Just For Whites............?

What Ever Happened To:
The Bill Of Rights
My Civil Rights And My Equal Rights?

So....... You Want Your Country Back.
Then, Give Me My Democracy Back.

Too Many Guns In The Street,
Too Many People Getting Beat.......

Mothers Crying, Cause
Their Babies Are Dying.

Government Denying,
That They've Been Spying.

We Got Too Many Wars.........
Killing Our Girls And Boys.

Afghanistan And Iraq,
Needs To Stop.................

Can't You Keep, Your Guns On The Rack?
Let Me Have My Democracy Back.

You Think You Lost Your Country
Because The President's Black,
Yea...... I Said It....... You Can't Change That.

He Didn't Make It.
He Didn't Take It.
He Didn't Break It.
What's The Matter With You
Can't You Take It?

Are You Too Blind?..... Can't You See?....Maybe
You're Just To Busy, Trying To Hate On Me.

The Fat Cats Are Killing
Your American Dream.

If You Don't Have No Money ,
Tell Me What Does That Mean?

No Minimum Wage, Darker Days, No Food
On The Table, You're living Like Slaves.

Is That What's In, The Master Plan………
To Get Rid Of The Black And The Tan.

Can't You See?............
The Poor and The Middle Ain't Free…
The Billionaires Have Taken, Your
DE-MO-CR-A-CY.

Stop All That Yacka-De-Yak...
We Need To Take Our Democracy Back.

Now The Moral Of This Story Is Plan To See.
The Fat Cats Are Hating On You And Me

It's All About The Money,
And The Power And Stuff.

We Need To Let The Suckers Know,
That We Have Had Enough.

Let's Put This Train Back On The Track.
Let's Take Our Democracy Back.

Author Melvin Hughes
Copyright © 4/24/2014

I'M IN LOVE WITH YOU AMERICA
BUT YOU WON'T LOVE ME BACK

You Forced Me Into Marriage
With You, A Long, Long Time Ago.
You Brought Me To This Land Of Yours,
That I Didn't Even Know.

I Had No Reason To Love You Then,
As I Listened To Your Whip Crack,
Yet I Do Love You America,
But You Won't Love Me Back.

You Made Me Work In Your Hot Fields,
Till I Thought My Back Would Break.
The Hours Were Long And Hard For Me...
And My Whole Body Ached.

I Nursed Your Kids And Sang You Songs,
And You Were Pleased With That.
I Really Love You America,
You Just Won't Love Me Back.

I Washed Your Clothes, Plowed Your Fields.
I Cared For Your Live Stock.
I Worked So Long And Hard For You....
I Thought That I Would Drop.

I Mended Fences, Served Your Meals.
I Laid Your Railroad Track.
I Do Love You America,
Why Won't You Love Me Back?

You Raped Me; You Beat Me...
You Took My Dignity.
You Robbed Me Of Every Thing I Had.
You Made A Slave Of Me.

You Stole My Great Inventions, And
I Wrote Great Music In Spite Of You.
I Tried To Make You Proud Of Me
In Everything I'd Do.

You Have Shown Your Hate For Me,
In Every Deed And Act.
God, How Much I Love You...
If You'd Only Love Me, Back.

You Gave Love To Germans,
The Italians, And The Jews,
The Japanese, The Dutch, The French;
You Loved The Irish Too.

I Wondered All These Many Years,
When You'd Give Love To Me.
I'd Fall In Love With Someone Else,
But You Won't Set Me Free.

Some Say That You're Afraid,
That If I Don't Behave...
I'll Become The Master And
You'll Become The Slave.

It Seems You Only Need Me,
To Have One To Look Down On.
You Certainly Do Not Treat Me,
As Though I Am Your Own.

I Want An Education...
A Job ... A Better Life.
When I try To Reach That Goal
I Find, You've Added To My Strife.

Why Do You Withhold Love From Me,
Because My Skin Is Black.
Could It Be That You're Afraid Of Me?
Are You Afraid To Love Me Back?

I've Fought In Wars Abroad For You,
Till Victory Was Won.
When You Had Used Me To Your Good,
You Left Me All Alone.

You've Perpetrated Crimes On Me
While Wearing Your White Sheets.
You Even Set Your Dogs On Me
And Killed Me In Your Streets.

You've Killed Those Who Would Give
I Love... Abraham, Martin, And John;
They All Took Me For Who I Am
its Sad That They Are Gone.

Perhaps Someday America
You'll Find Courage You Now Lack,
And You'll Find It In Your Heart
Someday, To Give Me Your Love Back.

But I Will Be What I Will Be,
And Let Me State This Fact;
You'll Soon Look Back
With Deep Regret_____

Because…..You Wouldn't Love Me, Back.

Author Melvin Hughes
Copyright © 08/15/2005

YES YOU CAN

You Think That You Can't Do It.
There Really Is Nothing To It.
You Just Keep Right On Pushing.
Yes, You Can.

Yes, The Mountain Is Real High,
It Almost Reaches To The Sky.
But I Know You Can Climb It.
I Know You Can.

Sure The Going Is Tough,
And The Road Is Rough.
You Just Run On To The End.
I Bet You Can.

No Matter What The Weather,
You Just Keep It All Together.
I Know That You Can Make It.
Believe That You Can.

Through The Rain And The Storm,
You Just Keep Pressing On
You Get That Prize At The End.
Everybody Knows That You Can.

It 'S Not As Long As It Seems,
You Just Keep Following That Dream.
You Can Reach The Final Goal.
You're A Winner And You Can.

When You've Climbed The Mountain,
And Weathered The Storm.
You've Won The Race And Are Moving On.
Aren't You Glad That You Kept Saying
to yourself... Yes, You Can!

Author Melvin Hughes
Copyright © 10/22/05

I KNOW MY SAVIOR LIVES

HE WAS BORN IN A LOWLY MANGER,
OUR CHRIST THE BABY CHILD.
HE CAME TO SPEND SOME TIME ON EARTH,
TO TARRY JUST A WHILE.

HIS HEART WAS FULL OF WONDROUS LOVE,
AS MIRACLES HE PREFORMED AND,
HE HAD NOT REACHED THE PINNACLE
OF THE REASON HE WAS BORN.

HE DIED UPON THE CROSS THAT DAY,
FOR YOUR SINS AND FOR MINE.
AND THEN WENT TO HIS FATHER,
BUT ONLY IN GOD'S TIME.

SURELY HE IS RISEN,
AND IS LIVING IN MY SOUL,
FOR YET TODAY, HIS LIFE AND TIMES
ARE EVER BEING TOLD.

I KNOW MY SAVIOR LIVES, AND,
HE ROSE ON EASTER MORN,
SO THE PROPHECY WAS FILLED,
FOR THIS PURPOSE HE WAS BORN.

I DON'T KNOW ABOUT YOUR SAVIOR,
BUT, DO I KNOW, ABOUT MINE.
I KNOW MY SAVIOR LIVES,
AND HE IS WITH ME ALL THE TIME.

AUTHOR MELVIN HUGHES
COPYRIGHT © 3/24/07

ST LOUIS

HAVE YOU EVER BEEN TO ST LOUIS?

MAN IT IS SOME KINDA TOWN.

IT'S JUST FULL OF PARTY PEOPLE,

AND WE REALLY KNOW HOW TO GET DOWN.

THERE'S THE GATEWAY ARCH,

AND THE ST LOUIS ZOO.

THE ST LOUIS CARDINALS,

THE RAMS AND THE BLUES.

THIS TOWN, IS FILLED WITH MUSIC,

THE BEST MUSIC IN THE LAND,

FROM COUNTRY AND JAZZ,

TO ROCK AND ROLL,

AND WORLD'S GREATEST BLUES BANDS.

THE FOOD HERE IS JUST SCRUMPTIOUS,

YOU JUST NAME YOUR OWN MENU.

IT'S ALL HERE IN ST LOUIS,

SERVED DAILY, JUST FOR YOU.

SO IF YOU'RE EVER LOOKING,

TO HAVE A REAL GOOD TIME.

JUST COME ON IN TO ST LOUIS, THAT'S

JUST WHAT YOU'RE GOING TO FIND

Author Melvin Hughes
Copyright © 11/14/05

GOOD MORNING MR. PRESIDENT

GOOD MORNING MR. PRESIDENT.
TELL ME. HOW ARE YOU TODAY?
I KNOW THAT YOU ARE BUSY SIR,
BUT I HAVE SOME THINGS TO SAY.

I KNOW YOU MUST GET STARTED,
BUT, JUST LISTEN IF YOU WILL,
SOMEBODY NEEDS TO TELL YOU
SIR, JUST HOW THE PEOPLE FEEL.

WE KNOW THE JOB YOU'RE DOING,
IS RIDDLED WITH STUMBLING BLOCKS,
BUT WE ARE HERE TO TELL YOU, THAT,
WE DON'T WANT YOU TO STOP.

YOU WANT GOOD JOBS... SO DO WE.
YOU WANT TO KEEP US SAFE TODAY.
WE KNOW YOU WANT,
HEALTH CARE FOR ALL,
AND YOU WANT IT RIGHT AWAY.

YOU WANT THE MIDDLE CLASS TO GROW,
AND PROSPER IN THIS LAND.
WE KNOW YOU WANT TO HELP THE POOR,
SIR... PLEASE DO THAT IF YOU CAN.

MOST OF US ROOT, FOR YOUR SUCCESS,
BUT SOME WANT YOU TO FELL.
THERE ARE SOME FOLKS, WHO DESPISE
YOU, AND WISH YOU WERE IN JAIL.

WHY...? WHERE DID IT ALL COME FROM?
THIS HATE THEY FEEL FOR YOU.
YOU WERE ELECTED, FAIR AND SQUARE,
NOT JUST ONE TIME BUT TWO.©©

THE FIRST BLACK MAN TO HOLD YOUR JOB,
SHOULD BE CELEBRATED BY ALL.
BLACKS, WHITES AND EVERYONE,
WE SHOULD ALL BE STANDING TALL.

IT PAINS ME SIR, TO SEE SUCH HATE,
FOR THE COLOR OF YOUR SKIN.
THE CONTENT OF YOUR CHARACTER,
SHOULD BE, WHAT MATER IN THE END.

YOUR JOB APPROVAL WOULD BE BETTER.
IF IT WASN'T FOR YOUR RACE,
I KNOW WE'D ALL BE BETTER SERVED,
IF IT WAS NOT FOR ALL THIS HATE.

HISTORY, WILL LONG REVEAL,
THE THINGS YOU COULD HAVE DONE,
AND HOW MUCH BETTER, WE COULD HAVE
BEEN, IF THE RACISM WAS GONE.

WELL...
I'VE TAKEN TOO MUCH OF YOUR TIME SIR
BUT, YOU KNOW WE'VE GOT YOUR BACK...
AND WE ARE SO DAMN PROUD OF YOU
AND IT'S NOT, BECAUSE YOU'RE BLACK.

DON'T WORRY ABOUT YOU LEGACY,
BECAUSE, HISTORY WILL BE PLAN.

IT WILL SAY...

HE WAS THE FIRST BLACK PRESIDENT
OF THE UNITED STATES.
BARACK OBAMA WAS HIS NAME.

AUTHOR MELVIN HUGHES
COPYRIGHT © 5/24/2014

You Hurt Me

How much do I love you?

It's so hard for me to say.

But one thing I can say for sure,

It's getting harder every day.

Because You Hurt Me

At first when we became friends,

You were so gentle and kind.

But I still remember the first time,

That you broke this heart of mine.

You Really Hurt Me

You apologized, you even cried.

You said... never again.

I accepted your apology and you lied

But, I wanted us to be friends.

But You Hurt Me.

Soon we married and had two kids,

I was sure that things would change.

But, it didn't, you still beat me up.

And things just stayed the same.

I don't know why, but you hurt me.

Each time you say you're sorry,

And you beg me to come back.

I listen and say, I'll try again

But that didn't change the fact.

I Came Back And You Hurt Me

I've tried every way I know how,

To give you what you need.

I've cried, I've begged, I've pleaded,

But nothing would success.

Man, You Hurt Me Bad

I have asked you to seek counsel,

I've even offered prayer.

I've done everything I know to do,

Except get out of here.

Can't you see? You hurt me.

Now I have no more choices,

I have to leave today.

I know that you will kill Me Soon,

If I don't get away.

You Love Me But You Hurt Me

No more coving up my black eyes,

And making excuses for you.

I'll listen to those who see me,

And do what I have to do.

Because, All The Time You Hurt Me

I Pray That You Get Help Someday.

I hope that you can see

I had no choice

I had to be free,

Because, You Kept On Hurting Me

AUTHOR MELVIN HUGHES
COPYRIGHT © 5/30/2014

ABOUT THE AUTHOR

Mel Hughes was born in 1940, in Kinloch, which is a suburb of St. Louis, Mo. He is the youngest of (three girls and two boys) five children. The family was very close knit, but poor. Not destitute, but barely getting by.

Both parents worked and the children pitched in where they could. They were able to escape poverty and thus survived. His father was a plant worker and served for 20 years, as Chief of the town's all volunteer Fire department. His mother was a factory worker and retired as a seamiest in the garment industry.

Mel had always had a gift for music and the arts and; is a saxophonist, singer, songwriter, and poet who spent ten years as a professional musician. He is married and has five children.

After leaving the entertainment field, he held several jobs, one of which was in a steel mill where he worked for eight years as an electrician. When that plant closed in 1981, the country was in a deep recession and work was scarce so he entered college at the age of 42, to expand his electrical skills.

While there, he studied electronics engineering technology, English Ligature, and writing. As a direct result of his college training, he was later employed at Washington University in St. Louis. From there he retired (in 2001) as a storeroom manager, after 11 years of service.

He was also a handyman, (a trait that he inherited from his father who could fix anything) so, three months after he retired from Washington University, he started a (in 2001, at the age of 61) company called "ODD JOBS INC" which he owned and operated until his second (2014) retirement.

Many times his work force was those unable to find work anywhere else, but who had marketable skills. These men were usually from homeless shelters and community help services. They could consist of homeless veterans, parolees and those who found themselves homeless and without jobs for a number of reasons.

They were always paid well, treated with dignity, and admired and respected by him and his clients. Some have even successfully reentered the work force. His company found that nitch between the homeowner and the contractor.

There was a need for someone who could complete jobs "Too Big for the home owner, but "To Small" for the contractor, so he put his "Handyman" skills to good use fulfilling that need, until his second, recent retirement. He felt that now; with time on his hands, he should "write that book". This book is meant to be, both spiritually uplifting and morally thought provoking.

BIOGRAPHY BY DARLEEN WILLIAMS

www.ingramcontent.com/pod-product-compliance
Lightning Source LLC
Chambersburg PA
CBHW060948040426
42445CB00011B/1055